The Resentment Cure

*How to Forgive
and Forget,
and Eliminate
the Resentment in Your
Relationship*

by Howard Cahill

Table of Contents

Introduction

No matter how happy your relationship is, you've probably experienced resentment at one point or another. Whether it was on your end or your partner's, the common denominator is that, most likely neither of you addressed it. In fact, either if not both of you may perhaps still be unaware of it. Resentment is something that can consume you entirely, and your relationship by extension, until there is nothing left.

I am here to tell you that it's not too late and that I have the *Resentment Cure* that you're looking for. Your relationship can be saved and you are, indeed, capable of forgiving, forgetting, and moving forward in your life. Yet, only *after* cleansing your heart and mind of any resentful feelings you might be holding on to.

It's not easy for everyone, but it's an attainable goal for the person who is invested and determined to improve their relationship and the quality of their own life. This can be done by letting go of the negative feelings that cast a shadow on potential happiness.

You have to be open to improvement, receptive to change and, of course, have the willingness to follow the necessary steps toward forgiveness. The secret is to look within yourself for clues, before you look at your partner. Ask yourself whether the source of your dissatisfaction is indeed your partner, or if it's a projection of some other factor that you're in denial about.

This book is designed to help you establish what the underlying issues are, and then take you through the steps of communication, expression, resolution, letting go of anger, forgiveness, and moving forward into a relationship that's more valuable and stronger than ever before. Let's get started!

Chapter 1: Introspection – Consider Whether Your Resentment Is Justified or Not

First and foremost, the process of eliminating resentment from your relationship calls for introspection. Before you take steps toward trying to forgive your partner for whatever shortcomings you may perceive in them, it is crucial to analyze yourself and your own feelings. Try to figure out exactly why you feel resentful of your partner. Is your resentment based on a series of actions on their part? Is it based on something they did or did not do, on something they said, or simply on something you *think* they did?

The most important question you need to ask yourself is: "Is my resentment justified?" An honest answer to that question will give you a pretty good idea of whether the problem lies in you, your partner, or the way both of you built your relationship.

If the answer is no, think about what makes you feel this way and why you're placing blame on your partner. Maybe it's that you feel inadequate and you're channeling your resentment onto them instead of working to solve your problem. Or perhaps there is something else happening in your life, and you're passive-aggressively directing your anger towards your partner instead of the person who really deserves it. Finally, you might be involved in a frustrating situation in your life, one that you can't solve, and because there's no one to blame, you project your resentment on your partner.

If your honest answer is 'yes,' the resentment is justified, it is important to realize in what area your partner is failing or not fulfilling your needs. Their failings can range from lack of attention, to disrespect, to more alarming things such as being unfaithful. In the worst case scenarios, they're verbally or physically abusive. Of course, while cheating may or may not be a deal-breaker, abuse should never be tolerated. If you experience verbal or physical abuse, immediately remove yourself from the dangerous situation and cut all contact with your partner.

Speaking of deal-breakers, you also need to figure out if what displeases you about your partner or their behavior is something intolerable for you. You need to decide whether or not you're able to continue a healthy relationship on these terms.

One of the most polarizing topics when it comes to relationship deal-breakers is cheating. It is one of the biggest sources of resentment between partners and one of the most dangerous when left unaddressed.

Not discussing it and reaching a conclusion about the situation together, whether it's continuing the relationship or breaking up, will absolutely breed resentment. In turn, this will lead to unhappiness and an even more bitter ending, in the long-run.

If cheating is something you will not stand for, be honest and realize the relationship has run its course. There's no point in further hurt for yourself and your partner by trying to keep something alive. If you can't forgive them and you're no longer able to see a future together, it's time to end it. Yet, maybe you are more lenient and willing to forgive, or think your partner's motives for betrayal were valid. Possibly, you believe it was a one-time thing and the misstep wasn't serious. In all of these cases, talk openly about what happened and discover your partner's reasons and feelings about it. You can come to a conclusion together, through healthy communication. While introspection and self-analysis is beneficial, pushing your feelings down is not. Only through open communication on both ends can you truly achieve a positive resolution of an inter-personal conflict and truly find the 'resentment cure'.

Chapter 2: Communicate with Your Partner About the Resentment

As with most things, this issue can be solved most efficiently by open, honest communication. In many cases, your partner might not even realize they are doing something wrong or that their attitude or behavior is a source of dissatisfaction and resentment for you. It's crucial that you are honest about your feelings, what is causing them and remain open to dialogue.

Be careful not to come off as overly accusatory – that will only cause your partner to become defensive and you won't be able to communicate effectively about what's bothering you. Explaining how you feel and listening to your partner doing the same are equally important in contributing to the positive resolution of your conflict. Communication goes both ways and remembering that will save you both resentment and heartache.

Explaining the way you feel and the ways in which your partner contributes to that is going to help them understand you. It will allow your partner the opportunity to put themselves in your shoes. This will encourage them to change their behavior accordingly. Or, they will explain their behavior and that they were un-aware of how you feel about it. As previously stated, careful listening on both parts is essential. A dismissive attitude or failure to take the issue seriously leads to even more unhappiness and buried emotions, which lead to resentment.

Again, it's important to phrase your feelings in the most non-accusatory way possible. But, at the same time, don't be shy to tell them when they're making you, or have made you, feel inadequate or uncomfortable and how that has contributed to your bitterness. Glossing over hurt feelings or sensitive issues will not help you solve the situation in any way. Furthermore, it is unfair both to you and your partner, who will not be able to change their attitude or improve the circumstances if they don't know the extent of the issue.

Try initiating the discussion at a time when you are both relaxed and not under stress or any kind of external pressure. Launching into a topic as heavy as this late at night, or when the two of you are tired or stressed from work is not going to lead to a constructive discussion or provide positive results. Instead, try approaching your partner in the morning or on a weekend - in a setting where they feel comfortable. Make sure there's plenty of time to talk; the last thing you want is to get into a fight before you go to work and then return home even more bitter and angry at each other. Give yourselves time to express how you feel, listen to each other and work things out.

Go into it with an open mind and trust that your partner is willing to compromise or admit their mistake and apologize. Making them aware of your feelings is going to lead to better results than holding it in. Getting rid of any misunderstandings that might have come between the two of you is a crucial step on the road to forgiveness and forgetting the problem ever happened. Honest communication is the number one solution to any issue between people, especially in a relationship. Forgiveness can't be reached without honest communication and without the willingness to give it.

Chapter 3: Expression Instead of Suppression

This chapter might as well have been called "Get Angry", because that's essentially what I'm advocating. I'm not saying to be angry all the time or for no reason, but when your feelings of anger or dissatisfaction are warranted, make sure to express them to your partner immediately and openly. Thoroughly explain why you feel this way. This ties in with our previous chapter about communication, but it is more about communicating on the spot, when the issue is relevant, rather than later.

Expressing your negative feelings is healthy and therefore makes your relationship healthier. Not wanting to appear negative causes you to repress your emotions. Repressing emotions, in turn, builds resentment, while expressing them gives you a chance to solve the issue effectively as it presents itself. When you openly express it leaves no room for latent feelings of anger that can build up and harm you and your relationship.

Think about it – voicing your irritation is liberating and negative feelings are just as valid as positive ones. You should never feel ashamed of being sad, angry, annoyed or any other way; feelings are meant to be expressed and not bottled up inside. Leaving negative feelings to accumulate inside means you're going to analyze and over-analyze them - picking them apart. It will cause you to remain angry for a much longer time than you necessary. Holding back builds frustration and makes you look at the situation in a non-objective way. This is not beneficial to anyone – not to you and not to your partner. All of those bad feelings turn into, you guessed it, long-term resentment.

In addition, not telling your partner how you feel may also be unfair to them and, in turn, make them feel like they have been lied to. Holding in resentment for a long time, only to voice it later on may also cause your partner to feel overwhelmed, confused and defensive. They're suddenly faced with a slew of accusations and hidden feelings that they've never been made aware of before - that's not an easy thing to handle. Actually, it is quite difficult, even for the most well-adjusted person, and it will prompt them to retaliate. This will undoubtedly escalate your conflict and make things worse than they already were.

Women are especially guilty of repressing their negative feelings, especially anger. This is because, in many cultures, girls are brought up to be complacent and accommodating to others and put themselves and their thoughts second. Paired with the ridiculous idea that anger is not "lady-like", repression does a lot of harm and no good. Men, on the other hand, are often 'allowed' and encouraged to express anger, as it's viewed as inherently masculine. Yet, many cultures ridicule men when it comes to expressing sadness or being 'emotional'. Men repress these type of feelings out of fear of appearing 'weak' or 'un-masculine', which doesn't do them any good, especially when it comes to relationships.

So, while repression is gendered, it is encouraged in both men and women for different reasons. It is also equally harmful to everyone, regardless of gender. Moreover, repressing emotions is never an effective tactic when dealing with inter-personal relationships. It is definitely a breeding ground for resentful feelings towards one another.

Forgiveness is more easily given and obtained by airing out feelings and clearing up the situation on the spot. Being honest and talking about your emotions is not detrimental, rather it's very helpful in diffusing a negative situation. If you let negative thoughts simmer for an extended period of time, it warps your view of things and causes reactions that are blown out of proportion.

Chapter 4: Let It Go and Move On

Once you have talked things out with your significant other and made the first steps toward a positive resolution of your issues, there's one absolutely crucial thing you need to do – let it go. In other words, once things are solved, stop dwelling on the past and move on with your life and your relationship.

True forgiveness can't be achieved without forgetting and that relies heavily on not thinking about the past. If you've decided to forgive and forget and communicated this to your partner, dwelling on your old negative feelings is unfair. It's unfair to both you and your significant other. Not only will it be detrimental to your own well-being, but to your entire relationship. If you keep thinking about all the reasons you resent your partner, even after you've talked about and resolved the issues, causes unnecessary pain. It only awakens your feelings of anger over and over again which is far from healthy for either of you. These feelings will eventually turn into new resentment and might ruin your relationship.

Making the decision to forgive and forget signals a mature, balanced individual. In keeping with that maturity and balance, you need to realize you'll never eliminate your feelings of resentment without first eliminating the cause. If you've reached this step, it means you've already successfully identified the cause of your displeasure and acted accordingly by talking to your partner about it. So, now that you have attended to the root of the issue and diffused the situation, the tension should be eliminated. At this point, the most difficult steps have already been completed.

However, it doesn't mean that the current step, to forgive and forget, is easy or any less important than the others. Each and every step is invaluable to your goal of letting go of your feelings of resentment - none can be skipped.

We all know that moving on is easier said than done. While we know that feelings arise on their own and cannot always be controlled - you *can* control how you react to the feelings or the issues that trigger them.

It may sound like a difficult and complicated process, but it's not impossible. You just have to make the conscious decision to not think about what triggered the negative feelings – don't allow them to upset you. Like all things, it's harder in the beginning, but gets easier with time and practice. You will get more and more used to responding to certain things in a different way than in the past. Once you rationally understand that you've already resolved the problem with your partner and overcame your negative feelings, it will be easier to control your emotional response.

Will power is a key strength here - along an honest desire to improve your relationship and truly forgive your significant other. Letting go of your old anger is liberating for you, as an individual, and will do wonders for your relationship. Your positive attitude and willingness to compromise will lead to a better future for your relationship. Compromise is essential for a healthy relationship. Taking control of your emotional response will be one of the best things you've ever done for yourself and you'll no longer be a slave to your feelings, however irrational or warranted they are.

Chapter 5: Focusing On the Positive

The final part of your journey toward forgiveness doesn't deal with the past, but looks to the future - a brighter and happier one. It's a step for those who have forgiven and whose wounds have healed. Those who are ready to let go of the past and their negative feelings in order to concentrate on the positive.

Maintaining a positive attitude is a common piece of advice - one that is sometimes ignored. However, it's a highly important part of the healing process. I'm not saying that you have to transform your personality and suddenly become an optimist, if that's not who you are or want to be, but I'm talking about focusing on the positive aspects of your relationship.

The negative feelings you've managed to eliminate must be replaced by positive ones. I encourage you to make an effort to seek and identify your favorite things about your partner and your relationship with them. Remember the beginning - what about your partner attracted you in the first place and what ways have they played a positive role in your life? Think of the small things that made you fall in love with them and that still keep your relationship going. That old saying, "In with the good and out with the bad" is not without merit and it will be of great help in the recovery process.

After spending a certain amount of time with someone, we tend to take them for granted. We stop appreciating them to the same extent we used to or maybe we simply stop showing it. You start thinking that your partner just knows you appreciate them without you having to say it. This is a surefire way of breeding resentment because humans are emotional beings that need to feel loved and appreciated - solid proof in words and actions is always welcome. A continuous lack of expressing affection and appreciation along with going through a difficult period full of resentment, can make it hard to remember what made your relationship enjoyable in the first place. That's why it is important to make a conscious effort to not only forgive and forget your partner, but often communicate how much you appreciate them. This will actively lead to improving your relationship.

The truth is that we all need reassurance in all aspects of life, and even more so in a romantic relationship. A partnership must be sustained equally by both of partners involved and reassurance plays a major role in that. It reiterates trust, appreciation and affection in your relationship and proves that you have truly moved on from your conflicts toward a better future with your partner.

I cannot stress enough how important this is, especially for a couple who may be feeling a little insecure after going through an intense emotional period. The secret to bringing your relationship back to normal and preventing resentment to come in between, causing you to drift apart, is to constantly nurture your relationship. Take extra care to do this if you're experiencing a difficult period.

Conclusion

Resentment can be a veritable disease in a relationship and, unfortunately, it is one that gains depth and strength the longer it remains bottled up inside. You may even reach a point where you think the relationship can never return and put all the blame on your partner. This in turn deepens your resentment even more. You can easily see how this becomes a vicious circle that is very hard to break. However, that doesn't mean it's impossible.

An open heart and mind along with a sincere desire to forgive and forget is what you need to begin the journey toward eliminating resentment from your relationship. Moreover, a strong will and resilience is necessary to successfully complete the journey. It's not an easy task, but it's one that worth working for if the end goal is saving your relationship. The end of your journey will prove to be rewarding because you will come out of it as an improved individual who took charge of their negative feelings and made a conscious decision to save their relationship.

Having reached the end of it, you know how important each and every step is and how every single one is crucial to a successful, satisfying outcome. Improving yourself and changing how you react to your emotions is in your own control and it can definitely decide the future of your relationship. Change is not out of your reach and it's up to you to decide if you want to take the necessary steps to regain a healthy, happy relationship.

Solving issues with your partner is not only *possible*, but it doesn't even require specialized help. The guide for getting rid of your feelings of resentment is in your own hands and the only thing you really need is the desire to do it. You have learned to analyze yourself and understand your feelings, communicate effectively with your partner, express your feelings and let go of anger to focus on the positive. It's up to you now to put it all in practice and work toward resolving your conflicts with maturity, rationality and in a healthy way. You'll end up feeling liberated from resentment and gain a renewed, happier connection with your partner.

Finally, I'd like to thank you for purchasing this book! If you found it helpful, I'd greatly appreciate it if you'd take a moment to leave a review on Amazon. Thank you!

Made in the USA
Las Vegas, NV
06 January 2023

65106566R00020